THE
BOOK OF...

W9-ARI-637

DINOSAURS

KINGFISHER
NEW YORK

KINGFISHER
LONDON & NEW YORK

Copyright © Kingfisher 2012
Published in the United States by Kingfisher,
175 Fifth Ave., New York, NY 10010
Kingfisher is an imprint of
Macmillan Children's Books, London.
All rights reserved.

Written and illustrated by Dynamo Ltd.
Concept by Jo Connor

Distributed in the U.S. and Canada by Macmillan,
175 Fifth Ave., New York, NY 10010

Library of Congress Cataloging-in-Publication data
has been applied for.

ISBN: 978-0-7534-6978-1

Kingfisher books are available for special promotions
and premiums. For details contact: Special Markets
Department, Macmillan, 175 Fifth Ave.,
New York, NY 10010.

For more information, please visit
www.kingfisherbooks.com

Printed in China
10 9 8 7 6 5 4 3 2 1
TTR/0512/LFG/140MA

WHAT'S IN THIS BOOK?

DINOSAURS . . .

HAVE YOU EVER WONDERED WHY... OR WHAT...OR WHEN?

It's natural to wonder about the world around us. It's a very complicated and surprising place sometimes. And you'll never understand what is going on around you unless you ask yourself a question every now and then.

We have investigated the prehistoric world to collect as many tricky dinosaur questions as we could find...

... and we also found the answers for you!

We now invite you to come with us on a journey around the world of dinosaurs so that we can show you all of the answers we have discovered.

We also thought it might be fun to see how much of this shiny new knowledge you can remember—so at the back of the book, on pages 56 and 57, you'll find some quick-quiz questions to test you. It's not as scary as it sounds—we promise it will be fun. (And, besides, we've given you all of the answers on pages 58 and 59.)

While we were searching for all of those answers, we found out some other pretty interesting things, too. We wrote them all down on these panels—so you can memorize these facts and impress your friends!

Are you ready for this big adventure?

Then let's go!

WHY AREN'T THERE ANY DINOSAURS AT THE ZOO?

Did you know . . .

Before people knew anything about dinosaurs, they thought that the dinosaur bones they found were the bones of giants or dragons.

Dinosaurs lived many millions of years ago. The last ones became extinct (died out) about 65 million years ago. Humans have been on Earth for only around two million years, so a human never met a living dinosaur, let alone put one in a zoo!

Did you know · · ·

Dinosaur remains are often found in many separate pieces that need to be put together like a big prehistoric jigsaw puzzle.

HOW DO WE KNOW ABOUT DINOS?

Some dinosaur bones have survived under the ground, and over millions of years they have slowly turned into stone fossils. When these are discovered and excavated (dug up carefully), experts can figure out what type of creature they belonged to.

DID DINOSAURS ALL LIVE AT THE SAME TIME?

Did you know . . .

The first dinosaurs were small and ran around on two legs. Over time, some types of dinosaurs grew much bigger and began to walk on four legs.

Dinosaurs lived on Earth for about 165 million years altogether. Over time, they evolved (changed gradually) so that different types of dinosaurs lived at different times, sometimes millions of years apart.

8

DO WE KNOW EVERYTHING ABOUT DINOS?

"Woof?"

There are still many things we don't know for sure about dinosaurs, such as what color they were or what noises they made. About ten new types of dinosaurs are discovered every year so we are gradually learning more.

Did you know . . .

Someone who studies fossils is called a paleontologist, (pay-lee-on-tol-oh-jist).

WHERE DID DINOS LIVE?

Fossils of dinosaurs have been found all over the world, but Earth looked very different when they were alive. Since the time dinosaurs lived, the land on the surface of this planet has changed position and new oceans and mountains have formed.

Did you know . . .

Dinosaur remains have been found near the South Pole. When dinosaurs lived, it was not a frozen wasteland as it is today. The weather was much warmer and there were many plants and animals living there.

WHO WERE DINOS' NEIGHBORS?

Did you know . . .

Dragonflies lived at the same time as dinosaurs, but they were much bigger than they are today. Their wings stretched up to 29 inches (75 centimeters) wide.

Flying and swimming reptiles lived on Earth at the same time as dinosaurs, who lived on land. There were also insects, fish, and small furry mammals that looked like rats.

DID DINOSAURS EAT ONE ANOTHER?

Did you know ...

Some dinosaur fossils have been found with injury marks on them, where the dinosaur was bitten or slashed during a fight.

Some dinosaurs were carnivores, which means they ate meat. These dinos hunted and ate prey (other animals). Other dinosaurs were herbivores, peaceful plant eaters who munched on vegetation all day long. There were also a few omnivores—dinosaurs that ate both plants and meat.

HOW CAN YOU TELL IF A DINO WAS SCARY?

Predators (hunting dinosaurs) had rows of sharp teeth, strong back legs for running fast, and long claws for fighting. Plant-eating dinosaurs had smaller, blunter teeth for grinding up vegetation, or sometimes a beak instead of teeth.

Did you know ...

Fierce Tyrannosaurus rex (tie-ran-oh-saw-rus rex) had sharp teeth as long as bananas and a bite three times more powerful than a lion's!

WERE DINOSAURS COLORFUL?

We do not know for sure what color every dinosaur was. It is very rare to find fossilized dino skin, but some dinosaur remains have been found with fossilized feathers, and scientists can test these to figure out what color they were. It turns out that some of these feathers were colorful.

Did you know . . .

The most colorful feathered dinosaur found so far is called Anchiornis (an-kee-or-nis). It had a red head and black-and-white striped feathers on its arms and legs.

WHAT WAS DINOSAUR SKIN LIKE?

Dinosaurs were a type of animal called a reptile. Their skin was scaly and wrinkly, like modern reptiles such as crocodiles and lizards. It would have been tough and hard to bite through.

Did you know . . .

Some dinosaurs had feathers. Experts think it is possible that, in certain cases, they might have evolved into birds.

WHAT DID DINOSAURS SOUND LIKE?

Dinosaurs might have made noises like modern crocodiles. Crocs make coughing, hissing, and bellowing sounds when they are communicating with their family or scaring off enemies.

WHICH DINOS HONKED THROUGH THEIR HEADS?

Did you know . . .

Hadrosaurs might have honked to one another to warn of danger or to impress a mate. Animals do the same things today.

Duck-billed dinosaurs, called hadrosaurs (had-row-sawrs), had a long, bony head crest. Inside the crest were hollow tubes, and it is possible that the dinosaurs blew through these, using the crest like a musical instrument to make honking noises.

VERE ALL DINOSAURS HUGE?

Did you know . . .

The smallest dinosaurs we know of measured about 12 inches (30 centimeters) long. These tiny creatures ran around like birds and even had feathers.

Some dinosaurs were the biggest creatures that have ever lived on land, but others were as small as chickens. The tallest ones were plant eaters, with very long necks for reaching high up into trees. They were a group of dinosaurs called sauropods, and some of them could reach as high as a modern five-story building.

WHO WAS THE HEAVIEST DINO?

Did you know . . .

Amphicoelias would have had to eat hundreds of pounds of plants every day, and was big enough to push over whole trees.

Tons

Amphicoelias (am-fi-seel-ee-as) is the heaviest dinosaur we know of. It probably weighed about 110 tons—roughly the same as 20 African elephants. It would have shaken the ground as it walked.

DID DINOSAURS HAVE HANDS?

Did you know . . .
A set of fossilized dinosaur footprints was found in Utah. A dinosaur called Dilophosaurus (dye-low-foh-saw-rus) may have made them when it walked in mud by a lake, 198 million years ago.

Dinosaurs that walked on two legs had forelimbs— short arms that ended in long fingers with claws on the ends. These were not like human hands but looked more like bird feet. A dinosaur would have used them for fighting or for gathering food.

DID DINOSAURS HAVE TOES?

Did you know . . .

The biggest dinosaur footprints ever found belonged to a sauropod (saw-row-pod). This giant plant eater's footprints measured up to 6.5 feet (2 meters) across.

Two-legged dinosaurs had long toes with sharp claws on the end for slashing their enemies. Four-legged dinosaurs had legs and feet more like an elephant's, with short, fat toes and rounder claws.

21

WHO WAS THE BIGGEST HUNTER?

Did you know . . .

Spinosaurus could arch its back, perhaps to spread out its back fin like a giant fan.

The biggest meat-eating dinosaur we know about is Spinosaurus (spy-no-saw-rus), which grew up to 49 feet (15 meters) long. It had long jaws like a crocodile's and a sail-like fin along its back that measured almost 6.5 feet (2 meters) high. The fin may have been for showing off or it may have worked like a radiator to help keep the dinosaur warm or cool.

WHO HAD THE LONGEST CLAWS?

Did you know . . .

Some two-legged hunting dinosaurs, such as Deinonychus (dye-non-ik-us), could flick out the claws on its feet, like switchblades. The name "Deinonychus" means "terrible claw."

A two-legged, plant-eating dinosaur called Therizinosaurus (thair-ee-zeen-oh-saw-rus) had three incredible, 3-feet-long claws on each forearm, a lot like curved swords. Although these claws looked vicious, the dinosaur probably mostly used them for pulling down tree branches to get at tasty leaves.

WHO **WAS** THE STRANGEST-LOOKING DINO?

It is hard to choose between Therizinosaurus, with its 3-feet (1 meter)-long claws, shaggy coat, and big fat belly, and Incisivosaurus (in-size-iv-oh-saw-rus), a cross between a bird and a lizard, with its giant teeth sticking out of its mouth!

WHO HAD A NOISY TAIL?

The giant plant-eating dinosaur Diplodocus (dih-plod-oh-kus) could swish its tail very quickly like a whip. The tail might have made a very loud cracking noise that would have scared off enemies.

COULD DINOSAURS SWIM?

Did you know . . .

Liopleurodon (lie-oh-ploor-oh-don) was the biggest giant reptile of the prehistoric oceans. It grew up to 49 feet (15 meters) long and was a terrifying hunter.

Dinosaurs were land animals, although some of them might have been able to swim short distances. If they did, they risked being eaten by the fierce swimming reptiles that lived in the oceans in prehistoric times. Some of these were as big as whales, with huge jaws and sharp teeth.

COULD DINOSAURS FLY?

Did you know...

One of the largest pterosaurs ever found was Quetzalcoatlus (ket-sal-co-at-lus). It had a wingspan of 36 feet (11 meters)—wider than a hang glider.

Dinosaurs could not fly, but pterosaurs (ter-oh-sawrs) could. They were flying reptiles that lived at the same time as dinosaurs. They had wings made of thin skin, like a bat's wings. Their jaws were long and pointed like beaks, and some had sharp teeth.

WHO WAS THE FASTEST DINO?

Struthiomimus (strooth-ee-oh-my-mus) had long, thin legs like an ostrich's, and it could probably run up to 50 mph (80kmph)—almost as fast as a racehorse. It may have needed to run to escape its enemies.

Did you know . . .

Scientists have figured out how fast dinosaurs moved by measuring the spaces between their footprints. Many dinosaurs who left footprints moved no faster than a person walking.

COULD DINOSAURS CLIMB TREES?

Some dinosaurs could probably climb. A feathered dinosaur called Microraptor (my-crow-rap-tor) had curved claws like a squirrel's that might have helped it grip branches.

Did you know . . .

Early on in dinosaur times, there were no grasses or flowering plants and few trees. But gradually, over millions of years, thick forests grew across parts of Earth.

DID DINOSAURS LIVE IN FAMILIES?

Some plant-eating dinosaurs lived in big herds, like modern animals do on the plains of Africa. Hunters might have lived together in small family groups, like wolves or lions do today.

Did you know . . .

We know that plant eaters often lived in herds because they have left behind fossilized footprint trails, made by many animals moving together.

DID DINOSAURS HAVE HOMES?

Did you know . . .

Many pterosaurs (flying reptiles) ate fish, so they lived by lakes or on seaside cliff tops, like modern water birds do.

NESTING SITE

CAFÈ

Most dinosaurs probably did not have one particular home. They may have migrated, which means that they moved to different places at different times of the year. However, they did sometimes have special nesting sites where the females went to lay their eggs.

WHO LAID THE BIGGEST EGGS?

A plant eater called Hypselosaurus (hip-sell-oh-saw-rus) laid the biggest dinosaur eggs we know about. Each egg was almost 12 inches (30 centimeters) long and 10 inches (25 centimeters) wide—about as big as 73 chicken eggs put together.

Did you know . . .

Hypselosaurus did not make a nest, but it might have buried its eggs in sand, like a turtle does.

WHAT DID DINO NESTS LOOK LIKE?

Did you know . . .

Dinosaurs often nested together in big groups. In Montana, at a site called Egg Mountain, experts have found many fossilized eggs and babies from different dinosaurs.

Many dinosaurs built nests by scraping a hollow circle in the ground, with a rim of earth around it. When they had laid their eggs, they piled layers of earth or plants on top to keep them warm.

WHAT WERE DINOSAU BABIES LIKE?

Baby dinosaurs were tiny versions
of their parents. Life would have
been very dangerous for them
until they grew big enough
to fight or to run away
from hungry hunters.

Did you know . . .

Baby dinosaurs chipped
their way out of their
eggs, just like baby
birds do today.

WHICH DINOS LOOKED AFTER THEIR BABIES?

A plant-eating dinosaur called Maiasaura (ma-ee-ah-sawr-ah) was a good mother. Fossilized females have been found near their babies. They were probably looking after them until they grew big enough to live on their own.

Did you know . . .

The name Maiasaura means "good mother lizard." These mothers probably protected their babies from fierce predators.

HOW BIG WAS DINO POOP?

Dinosaurs have left behind fossilized poop. Scientists call these pieces coprolites. The biggest one found so far was 17 inches (43 centimeters) long. It may have come from a Tyrannosaurus rex. Plant eaters produced a lot of droppings, like modern cattle do.

Did you know . . .

Scientists can tell whether dinosaurs ate plants or animals by studying their fossilized poop.

HOW WELL COULD DINOSAURS SMELL?

Dinosaurs had big nostrils and a long muzzle (nose and mouthparts), so they probably had a good sense of smell. Meat eaters might have had the best sense of smell though, because they had to find prey.

Did you know . . .

Tyrannosaurus rex had a very large muzzle, probably to sniff out its food.

DID DINOSAURS LIKE TO SUNBATHE?

Did you know . . .

Humans are warm-blooded, which means we can create some body heat of our own. Modern reptiles are cold-blooded. They need to get heat from the sun to keep their bodies warm.

People once thought that dinosaurs were cold-blooded. This means that they needed the sun to help them keep their bodies warm, like modern snakes and lizards do. Now it is thought that they might have been warm-blooded, so they would have been able to live in cold places as well as warm ones.

DID DINOSAURS LIVE IN COLD PLACES?

Some dinosaurs lived in places where it was cold and dark in the winter. They probably ate as much as they could in the summer and lived off their body fat in the winter, like bears do today .

Did you know . . .

A dinosaur called Troodon (tro-oh-don) lived in the far north of the world. It had feathers to keep it warm and big eyes that helped it hunt in the dark, like a modern owl does.

DID DINOSAURS WEAR ARMOR?

Some dinosaurs had very tough, bony plates on their bodies, like armor. Some had spikes and horns, too, to defend themselves from hungry attackers.

Did you know . . .

Ankylosaurus (an-ky-low-saw-rus) was like a dino tank! It had armor-plated skin, spikes and horns, and a big club on the end of its tail, like a giant hammer.

WHO WAS THE SPIKIEST DINO?

Did you know . . .

It's possible that dinosaurs with long neck spikes could crash them together to make a frightening noise.

A plant eater called Edmontonia (ed-mon-toe-nee-ah) had the most spikes. They were on its neck, shoulders, and sides. It might have charged like a rhino when it was threatened by enemies.

DID DINOS HAVE GOOD EYESIGHT?

Dinosaurs probably had good eyesight to help them hunt for food. But nobody knows what color their eyes were or if the irises (the black centers of the eyes) narrowed to slits in bright light, like a cat's eyes do.

Did you know . . .

Troodon had the biggest dino eyes we know about. They were 1.8 inches (4.5 centimeters) wide—about the same size as an ostrich's eye.

COULD DINOSAURS SEE IN THE DARK?

Some dinosaurs had night vision. Velociraptor (veh-loss-ee-rap-tor), a vicious hunting dinosaur, might have been a nighttime hunter. To stay safe, plant eaters may have rested in herds, taking short naps while others stayed awake and could warn of nighttime danger.

WERE DINOSAURS THIEVES?

Some dinosaurs probably stole and ate the eggs of other dinosaurs. Birds and lizards steal eggs in a similar way today.

Did you know . . .

Stegosaurus's back plates might have been brightly colored to attract other Stegosauruses.

Many dinosaurs had body parts that were probably used for showing off in order to attract mates. Some had head crests, sails, or big plates on their backs. A dinosaur called Stegosaurus (steg-oh-saw-rus) had the biggest back plates, sticking up at least 27 inches (70 centimeters) high.

HOW WERE DINOSAUR FOSSILS MADE?

Dinosaur bones could become fossilized if they were buried under layers of sand or mud, perhaps in a lake or river, many millions of years ago. Over time, the bones would gradually harden or leave traces of their shape.

Did you know . . .

Not all fossils are dinosaur bones. Fossilized plants have been found, too, and even leaves with dinosaur bite marks on them!

WHERE IS THE BEST PLACE TO FIND A FOSSIL?

Fossils are found only in a type of crumbly, sandy stone called sedimentary rock. Cliffs and rocky deserts are usually made of sedimentary rock, and fossils are often found in these areas.

Did you know . . .

At Ghost Ranch in New Mexico, experts found the biggest number of dinosaur fossils ever. Hundreds of small meat-eating dinosaurs called Coelophysis (see-low-fye-sis) died there, perhaps killed by a volcanic eruption.

WHICH ARE THE BIGGEST DINO FOSSILS?

The biggest fossils are the bones of sauropods—giant plant-eating dinosaurs. For instance, a huge forearm was found in Spain measuring 5.84 feet (1.78 meters) long, the size of an average man! It may have belonged to a supersized sauropod called Paralititan (pah-ra-lih-tie-tan).

Did you know . . .

Dinosaurs often leave behind only one or two fossilized bones. Scientists have to try to figure out the size of a dinosaur from only a few remains.

WHICH IS THE SMALLEST FOSSIL EVER FOUND?

A neck bone measuring only 0.28 inches (7.1 millimeters) long, found in England, turned out to be a tiny piece of a small birdlike dinosaur called Maniraptoran (man-ee-rap-tor-an). Maniraptoran was probably about the size of a small chicken.

Did you know . . .

Scientists compare the pieces they find to other dinosaurs found around the world to see if they can match the sizes and shapes.

W AT WAS THE FIRST FOSSIL EVER FOUND?

Did you know . . .

At first, people thought that Megalosaurus walked on all fours, but we now know that it walked on two legs, like Tyrannosaurus rex did.

A hunter called Megalosaurus (meg-ah-lo-saw-rus) was the first fossil to be identified as a dinosaur. Parts of it were first discovered in the 1700s, and people at the time thought that it might belong to a giant human. It was finally recognized as a dinosaur in 1824.

WHO NAMED THE FIRST DINOSAUR?

A British fossil expert named William Buckland (born in 1784) was the first person to realize that the Megalosaurus remains were those of a giant lizardlike creature. He gave it the first-ever dinosaur name.

Did you know . . .

The name Megalosaurus means "great lizard."

WHY DO DINOSAURS HAVE LONG NAMES?

Did you know . . .

A dinosaur's name is often made up of the Latin words to describe how it looked or behaved. For instance, Oviraptor (oh-vee-rap-tor) means "egg thief."

TYRANNOSAURUS REX

STRUTHIOMIMUS

Dinosaur names are written in Latin, a very old language first used by the ancient Romans. Scientists use Latin to name all of Earth's creatures. That way, everyone around the world can use the same names.

WHICH DINOSAUR HAS THE LONGEST NAME?

Micropachycephalosaurus (mike-row-pak-ee-ceff-ah-loh-saw-rus) has the longest name of any dinosaur. It was a tiny plant eater, about 7 inches (17 centimeters) tall. Its name means "tiny thick-headed lizard."

Did you know . . .

The word "dinosaur" comes from the Greek words deinos ("terrible") and sauros ("lizard"). So dinosaur means "terrible lizard."

MICROPACHYCEPHALOSAURUS

WHAT HAPPENED TO DINOSAURS?

Sixty-five million years ago, many dinosaurs died out. Scientists think that the weather on Earth may have changed, so plants died and there was not enough food for the dinosaurs. This might have happened because large volcanoes erupted or because an asteroid from space hit Earth. We may never know for sure.

Did you know . . .

Small animals, such as mammals and insects, survived when dinosaurs died out. Perhaps they needed less food than dinosaurs.

COULD DINOSAURS COME BACK?

Did you know . . .

It is possible that some dinosaurs survived, evolved, and are living with us now as birds! What do you think?

In the story *Jurassic Park*, scientists bring dinosaurs back to life by copying their DNA—chemicals found in the cells of the body. In real life, nobody has found any dinosaur DNA—not yet. If we do find any, the DNA would probably be much too old to use.

QUICK-QUIZ QUESTIONS

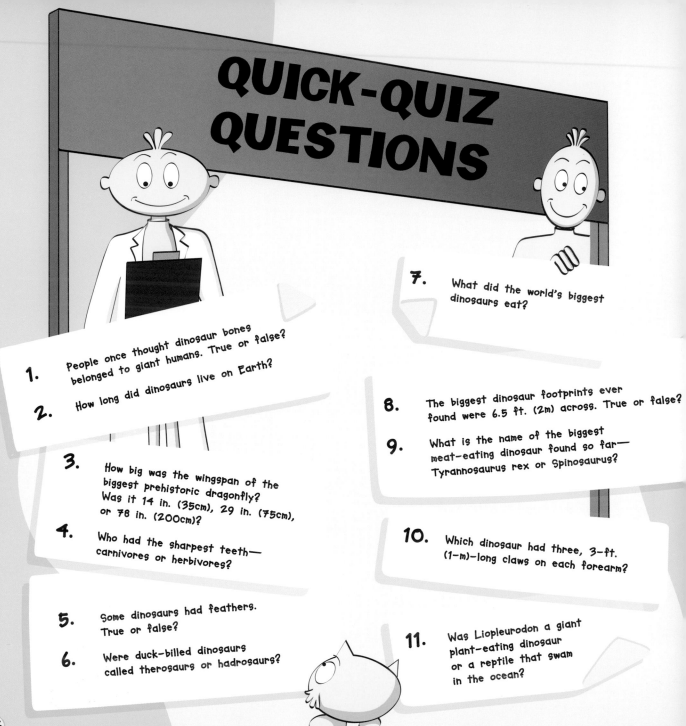

1. People once thought dinosaur bones belonged to giant humans. True or false?

2. How long did dinosaurs live on Earth?

3. How big was the wingspan of the biggest prehistoric dragonfly? Was it 14 in. (35cm), 29 in. (75cm), or 78 in. (200cm)?

4. Who had the sharpest teeth—carnivores or herbivores?

5. Some dinosaurs had feathers. True or false?

6. Were duck-billed dinosaurs called therosaurs or hadrosaurs?

7. What did the world's biggest dinosaurs eat?

8. The biggest dinosaur footprints ever found were 6.5 ft. (2m) across. True or false?

9. What is the name of the biggest meat-eating dinosaur found so far—Tyrannosaurus rex or Spinosaurus?

10. Which dinosaur had three, 3-ft. (1-m)-long claws on each forearm?

11. Was Liopleurodon a giant plant-eating dinosaur or a reptile that swam in the ocean?

12. Did Microraptor have curved claws for climbing trees or for swimming?

13. Some plant-eating dinosaurs lived in herds, like cattle do today. True or false?

14. Which dinosaur laid the biggest eggs that we know about?

15. Does the dinosaur name Maiasaura mean "good mother lizard" or "good baby lizard?"

16. Dinosaurs could not smell one another. True or false?

17. Did dinosaurs hunt only in daylight?

18. Did all dinosaurs have armor?

19. How do scientists figure out the size of a dinosaur's eye? Do they measure the eye socket or the eyeball?

20. Did Stegosaurus have plates or spikes along its back?

21. Is a fossil hard or soft?

22. How long was the neck bone of the tiniest dinosaur we know about? Was it 0.12 in. (3.1mm), 0.28 in. (7.1mm), or 0.6 in. (15.1mm) long?

23. Megalosaurus was the first dinosaur to be named. Does the name mean "long lizard" or "great lizard?"

24. Dinosaur names are written in which language?

25. How many years ago did dinosaurs die out?

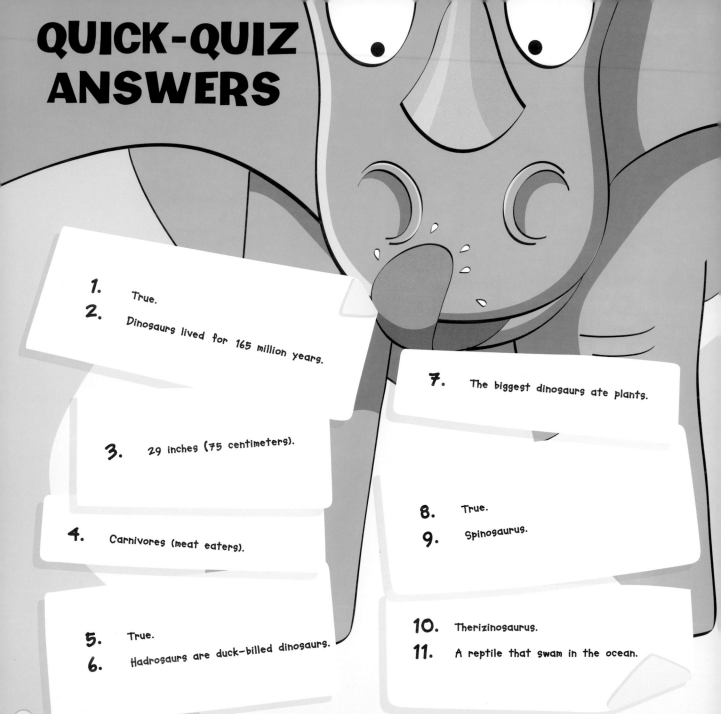

QUICK-QUIZ ANSWERS

1. True.
2. Dinosaurs lived for 165 million years.

3. 29 inches (75 centimeters).

4. Carnivores (meat eaters).

5. True.
6. Hadrosaurs are duck-billed dinosaurs.

7. The biggest dinosaurs ate plants.

8. True.
9. Spinosaurus.

10. Therizinosaurus.
11. A reptile that swam in the ocean.

12. For climbing trees.

13. True.

14. Hypselosaurus.

15. Good mother lizard.
16. False, they could smell one another.

17. No, some probably hunted at night.

18. No, not all had armor.
19. They measure the eye socket.

20. Plates.

21. Hard.
22. 0.28 inches (7.1 millimeters).

23. Megalosaurus means "great lizard."

24. Latin.
25. 65 million years ago.

TRICKY WORDS

ASTEROID
A large piece of rock that hurtles through space. Asteroids sometimes crash into planets.

CARNIVORE
An animal that eats only meat.

COPROLITE
The scientific name for fossilized dinosaur poop.

CREST
A ridge on top of a dinosaur's head made of hornlike material.

DINOSAUR
A Latin word meaning "terrible lizard" and the name given to the many different reptiles that lived on land between 230 and 65 million years ago.

DNA
A set of chemicals inside each cell of a living creature.

EVOLUTION
The process by which creatures adapt gradually to their environments and change shape, size, and behavior over millions of years in order to ensure they survive.

EXCAVATE
To dig out carefully from the ground.

EXTINCT
When a type of creature dies out and none of its kind are left.

EYE SOCKET
A bony, round hole in the head of a skeleton, where the eyeball fits.

FOSSIL
The remains of a plant or animal preserved in rock.

HADROSAUR
A dinosaur that had a mouth shaped like the beak of a duck.

HERBIVORE
A creature that eats only plants.

LATIN
An ancient language used by scientists to name all living things.

MAMMAL
A warm-blooded animal, with hair or fur, that drinks its mother's milk when it is born. Humans are mammals.

MIGRATE

To move from one region or habitat to another—for example, as the seasons change

NIGHT VISION

Eyesight that is adapted to see in the dark. Cats have night vision.

OMNIVORE

A creature that eats both plants and animals.

OVIRAPTOR

A birdlike, hunting dinosaur with feathers.

PALEONTOLOGIST

A scientist who studies dinosaur remains.

PREDATOR

An animal that hunts other animals to eat.

PREHISTORIC

Describes the period of history before our written records began.

PREY

An animal that is hunted by other animals.

PTEROSAUR

A flying reptile that lived at the same time as dinosaurs.

REPTILE

An animal that has scaly skin and lays eggs.

SAUROPOD

A very large dinosaur that ate plants. Sauropods were the largest land animals that have ever lived.

SEDIMENTARY ROCK

A crumbly type of rock formed over millions of years from sand or mud. Fossils are found in sedimentary rock.

WHERE TO FIND STUFF

Wow! What an amazing journey! We hope you had as much fun as we did and learned many new things. Who knew there was so much to discover about dinosaurs? Here are some other exciting books in which you'll find more to explore:

The Book of . . . the Human Body
The Book of . . . How?
The Book of . . . What?
The Book of . . . Where?
The Book of . . . Which?
The Book of . . . Who?
The Book of . . . Why?

Look out for these great books!
"Who" knows "what"
we'll discover . . .

See you soon!